YOUNG

NO KIDDIN'

DURHAM AND CUMBRIA
1993

First published in Great Britain in 1993 by
POETRY NOW
1-2 Wainman Road, Woodston,
Peterborough, PE2 7BU

Contents

Jamaica

In Jamaica it's always hot,
But in the north east where
I come from.
It's sometimes cold and sometimes not.

They have ackee and salt fish,
We just have cereal in a big dish.

Laura Davies (11) Broom Cottages Primary School

Jamaica

Jamaica has a feast,
Unlike the ones in North East.
They have salt fish and jelly cakes,
Unlike the one's that my mama makes.

While their beaches are sunny,
Over here the rain is runny.
They only have one rainy season,
While were having gun powder treason.
Over there the sea is blue,
But here in England that isn't true.

Adell Walton (11) Broom Cottages Primary School

The Sunny Country

In the sunny country,
Jamaica is its name.
On Redhills road, Kingston,
It's warm all day.

But up in the north
Where we live
It's just a different thing,
Even when we think it's warm
They'll think it's cold.

In Jamaica there's dusty roads,
Ours are all tarmac,
They go to school early
And come home early too.

I wish I lived there
Where it's nice and warm,
With lots of tropical fruit,
Peaches, Mango, lots of fruit,
Picking in the hot days sun.

Helen Metcalfe (10) Broom Cottages Primary School

3

Jamaica

The north east is a cold wet miserable place,
Even in the summer it's cold and wet.
I wish I could live in Jamaica,
With the carpenters, tailor and bakers
All working in the street,
Their huts are too hot.
But over here in the north east
You never see people work in the street,
I would love to wake up and have a shower,
But in the north east you see great big towers,
I would love to wake up to akee and salt fish
I wish, I wish, I wish.

Phil Davy (11) Broom Cottages Primary School

Jamaica

In Jamaica it's very hot. Blue sky's
Always. Hot days always.
Dull here, hot there, always. Buses
here, buses there, buses everywhere.
Jamaica is hotter than here.
They have to hang onto buses. We don't.

Sean Stephenson (10) Broom Cottages Primary School

5

Darkness

The sun sets,
The darkness pours over the hills,
It spreads through the air
Devouring everything in its path.
It spreads like ink on blotting paper,
It steals the light away and replaces black emptiness.

Steven Hamilton (11) Cassop JM & I School

The Big Mess

In my bag the mould grows thick and green, long and short.
The stuff that causes that is
Wet swimming trunks from last year,
A big mouse that fell in the bubbling chip pan,
A big furry toe nail, I don't know what the fur is,
Part of an ear, a snail and a slug that slides over my big thirty cm
Ruler,
A pair of old football boots all covered in mud
And part of an old black filling that fell out when I was four.
All of the zips are rusty. They are really a mess.
And an old blob of gravy from last year's Christmas dinner.
Wait one moment, that
is not all, there is still the corners pocket yet to go.

In the corner pocket there is . . .

Part of an orange all covered in mould,
A rusty old nail all bent and bowed.

In the other pocket there is . . .

All my *PE* kit, never been washed
And used up tissues.
What a mess.

Oh and I mustn't forget Granny's slippers
And the note to my mam from the head teacher.

There is a lot of other things I could
Name, but I've forgotten the rest, so if you ask to look in
My bag and I
Showed you, you would wish hadn't. Your faces would turn
Geen and turn away.

My sports bag.

John Daniel Mather (10) Cassop J M & I School

Turtles

Frst an egg then a green
reptile crawling across the
the sandy beach,helpless
against all predators,foxes
crabs, they're all the same,
they know when the time is
right,they know when to pounce.

Michael Kirk (11) Cassop JM & I School

The Writer of this Poem

The writer of this poem is as tall as a house
and has a friend as short as a mouse.
I am the best music player in the world.

The writer of this poem is the only one that
has seen the stars and the universe.

The writer of this poem is the best dancer
in the world and the best singer in the whole world.

The writer of this poem can read books faster then
a robot and can flick through books as quick as lightning.

The writer of this poem is as cute as me and
a friend as good as can be. That's Kimberly.

Zoë Barnett (9) Cassop JM & I School

All my Own Stuff

It wobbles and you can eat it.
jelly, I like that stuff.

Grown ups by it and shops sell it.
Lager, I like that stuff.

Farmers get them and you can eat them.
Egg, I like that stuff.

It smells and it's sticky,
Glue, I like that stuff.

You put things in it and you can drink out of it.
Glass, I like that stuff.

You draw with it and it's made of wood.
Pencils, I like that stuff.

You make it and you can eat out of it.
Bowls, I like that stuff.

It's got lots of words in it and people use it.
A dictionary, I like that stuff.

Kimberly Smith (9) Cassop JM & I School

Flames

Slowly, golden yellow mountains build up
in the edges of the paper and move to
the centre, leaving nothing but black fragile paper
while they dance along, destroying everything
In their path like a mindless beast.
Finally it gets bored with nothing
to burn and goes out.

Ian Swainston (11) Cassop JM & I School

The Dragon Who Never was

I've got a dragon.
He is a big, big dragon.
He sits in the attic.
He eats and eats.
But he does not east food, he east dust.
That is what my dragon eats.
But grass and leaves are a treat for my dragon.

Lisa Holden (10) Cassop JM & I School

Stars

Dots of broken diamonds sellotaped onto a cool background.
A myriad of points of light in a galaxy of their own.
A glittering backgroud. Then the plough comes and ploughs it all

up.

The plough goes and the constellation of stars comes back.

Leanne Williamson (10) Cassop JM & I School

In my Sports Bag

In my sports bag I have a pair of sand shoes for PE.
A pair of green shorts which are silky.
A pair of normal shorts.
I have a pair of trainers, if I am not wearing them.
I always carry a shell suit
And sometimes a purse.
I have a recorder.
Now here is the disgusting stuff -
Old chewing gum which is stuck to my bag.
A dead green frog.
A squashed banana.
A dead mole.
A mouldy apple.

Gemma Robinson (10) Cassop JM & I School

Darkness

In bed I look out of my window and see the darkness
Come out of the ground. It seems that it is coming
Up to attack me.
In bed I look out of my window and see the darkness
Covering the beautiful colours.

Christopher Myers (9) Cassop JM & I School

Waking Up

In the morning my mum wakes me up,
I get ready and I get some cornflakes
For my breakfast.
I get my bag and go to school
And play in the yard.

Craig Race (10) Cassop JM & I School

The Dragon

Deep in a cave in the south of the country
A dragon lay snoring and grunting.
What that dragon's mouth was doing
I do not know, all I know is
Now the cave is no more.

Mark McDonnell (10) Cassop JM & I School

Playing Out

Before I go to the rec
My dad says I have to be back for six thirty.
I go down the street, turn left and the first street I come to I go up.
I call for Wayne then we walk up a little bit
Then we climb over a fence. The rec is a big field with bushes
                                                    at the side.
It is a good place to play because you make camps
In the bushes. Then I check my watch, it's time to go home.

Gareth Davies (9) Cassop JM & I School

Water

The brass tap turns like a windmill,
First a trickle then a flood.
The silver liquid streams down like a waterfall.
The bubbles like marbles on a glass table.
The soapy water stinging my eyes.
I wash my face, a white beard appears like an old man.
I quench my thirst with a mouthful of water.
Beautiful stuff, water.

Ben McManners (11) Cassop JM & I School

Me and Faye

Me and Faye like fishfingers and chips,
fishfingers and chips,
fishfingers and chips.
Me and Faye like fishfingers and chips,
we eat them all day.

Me and Faye like beefburgers and chips
beefburgers and chips,
Beefburgers and chips,
Me and Faye like beefburgers and chips,
we eat them all day.

Me and Faye like coleslaw and chips,
coleslaw and chips,
coleslaw and chips.
Me and Faye like coleslaw and chips,
we eat them all day.

Me and Faye were ill last night,
ill last night,
ill last night.
Me and Faye were ill last night,
so we'll never eat them again.

Nicola Robertson (9) Cassop JM & I School

Wings

If I had wings
I would fly to the stars.
If I had wings I would sleep on the clouds.
If I had wings I would breathe in the morning air.
If I had wings I would hold up the sun.

Danielle Simpson (10) Cassop JM & I School

Water

Water is very important.
Water trickles down my mouth and slides down my throat
Keeping my body in shape.
Water gets you clean.
There is hot water and cold water.
When washing machines are used one hundred litres
                                        of water is wasted.

Steven Peters (9) Cassop JM & I School

Ten Little Cassop Kids

Ten little Cassop kids walking in a mine, one fell in
and then there were nine.
Nine little Cassop kids fishing in a lake, one fell in
and then there were eight.
Eight little Cassop kids walking up to heaven, I could not
walk too much and then there were seven.
Seven little Cassop kids getting into a fix, one got kicked
and then there were six.
Six little Cassop kids diving in a pool, one got knocked out
and then there were five.
Five little Cassop kids playing with dough, one got tangled up
and then there were four.
Four little Cassop kids making a cup of tea, one got scolded
and then there were three.
Three little Cassop kids slipping down the loo,
and then there were two.
Two little Cassop kids jumping on a wall, one went too far
and then there was one.
One little Cassop kid crying in the corner, he got gobbled up
and then there was none.

Lindsey Adams (11) Cassop JM & I School

Scattery Has a Game of Netball

I don't know how the Dragon got in the team,
Probably cheated wildly,
The Dragon's a little litter bug,
Just like my little slug.
She broke the net
And bent the pole,
Bust the ball,
Fowled the game,
I'll never let her play again.

Emma Frost (9) St Josephs RC School

The Silver Shimmering Flakes

The night was cold and bitter.
Soft flakes gently falling down.
Beautiful frozen patterns lay upon the ground.
The soft feathery cover had just began to form.
I was glad I was in the house keeping very warm.

Outside the tree was covered from head to crooked toe.
The icy pond shimmered in the moonlight.
As I crept upstairs to snuggle down.
I was glad I was in my bed keeping very warm.

Ellen Vickerstaff (10) St Josephs RC School

Cold

Cold, very cold.
Lovely cold blossom.
When the wind blows
It whirls around you.

Andrew Robson (10) St Josephs RC School

Jack Frost

Pouncing up and down the garden
In his long white gown.
Sliding, jumping, the spirit moves,
Spreading his glitter 'til everything
Glows.

Nicola Glass (9) St Josephs RC School

My Shadow

My shadow follows me all around,
On the walls and on the ground,
In the park and on the trees,
He gets smaller when I'm on my knees.
He moves when I do.

He never hurts me, day or night,
But sometimes gives me an awful fright,
On the water, on the land,
Even when I'm in the sand.
He moves when I do.

He'll be with me wherever I go,
We are attached from toe to toe,
We'll be together for all of time,
Mostly in the sunshine.
He moves when I do.

Nichola Swankie (9) St Josephs RC School

The Dragon Who Lives Next Door

A dragon lives next door to to me, I know its very rare,
But if you don't believe me just take a look right there.
His skin is very scaly, his jaws are very wide
And if you're very nice to him, he'll give you all a ride.
He loves to play with children, he gives them rides across the sky
And if you're very frightened, he'll tell you not to cry.
A dragon lives next door to me, I know it's very rare
And if you're not very nice to him, he'll fly off in the air.

Eloise Harker (10) St Josephs RC School

Springing Snowflakes

Falling, spinning in the air,
Down come snowflakes from way up there.
There's a robin up very high
Like a crystal in the sky.
The wind is blowing the trees are bare.
The white is still here but nobody there.

Matthew Abraham (9) St Josephs RC School

A Cold Winters Night

On a cold winters night, it was chilled bright,
The stars twinkled
As the snowflakes fell.
The wind whistled through the trees
On a cold winters night.
On a cold winters night,
It was cold in the town and the leaves were rattling.
On a cold winters night.

Stephen Smith (9) St Josephs RC School

Why Kill the Earth

Was it you who dropped the petrol on the road,
Who killed the little bird
So innocent?
Was it you who poisoned the beautiful fish in the sea?
Just because you were bored,
Perhaps,
Or showing off to your friends.
Or maybe it was you who cut down the tree
To build the patio.
I think I would prefer fresh air
To a patio.
Wouldn't you?

Joanne Rigby (11) Benfieldside Junior School

Save our Earth

Save the animals, save the turf, save whatever is on the earth.
Save the Rainforests, save the trees, save what ever blows
                                                    in the breeze.
Save the dolphin, save the whale, save them all without fail.
Save the leopard, save it fast, save it now before it's the last.
Save them,
Save them,
Save them fast or the world may have no past.

John Herdman (11) Benfieldside Junior School

My Poem

Would you like to kill the sea with lots of animals in it?
Would you like to kill the land by pulling down our trees?
Would we become extinct?
Could we die of dirt in the water that has come from out rivers?
There would not be any animals left on our earth for us to look after.
Some people take advantage of our precious world.
Help to save our world or there will not be anything left of it.
We need to have a world, well
I would, I do not know about you.
I love the world, not like the people who are killing our plants.
people think that you can just click your fingers and up comes
Another tree.
Trees take lots of years to grow.
Healthy, happy atmosphere.
Let's have them back and we will cheer.

Claire Cook (11) Benfieldside Junior School

Save our Planet

Save our plant,
Save our birds,
Save our animals,
Or best of all save ourselves.
If we do not start saving the Earth
One of these days Earth's going to go bang.
Start cleaning up.
Start saving the Earth.
It's not too late yet.
But soon it will go bang.
So let's get together and start saving the Earth.
Save the whales from extinction.
Save the seals as well.
Start saving the Earth.
Use recycled things.
Recycle aluminium cans and clean up the Earth.
Don't drop litter.
Start protecting the ozone layer or soon we will not
                                        be able to breathe.
So save the Earth or it will come like Mars,
There once was life but now it's gone.

Stuart Alan Taylor (11) Benfieldside Junior School

Save our Earth

Our Earth is a small sphere,
compared to all the plants,
so why can't we keep it clean?
Don't destroy the trees,
it's not hard to keep a planet clean,
all where doing is destroying!

Don't harm the animals,
they haven't harmed us,
why do we kill them?
That's what bothers me,
just for money,
What a Waste!

Don't pollute the rivers,
it harms the ozone layer,
it pollutes the air we breathe in,
it kills the little fish,
it poisons animals that drink it,
which leads to their *Death!*

The trees are being destroyed,
people are cutting the trees down,
to make paper with,
we will run out of oxygen,
because the trees are being cut down,
Don't Destroy the Forests!

God made this planet for us,
look what we've done,
he has been nice to us,
we should be nice back,
we should clean up the mess,
Have we been Wise!

Stephanie Southwood (10) Benfieldside Junior School

36

The World is in Danger!

Do you want to live underground? I don't,
Do you want the world destroyed? I don't,
Do you want the whales extinct? I don't,
Do you want to be choked with pollution? I don't,
Do you want to wear a plastic suit when you go paddling? I don't,
Do you want to swim in the sea and not be polluted? I do,
Do you want all the wildlife of the sea dead? I don't,
If we don't look after our world and care for its animals, who will?
Do you want to see the rainforest destroyed? I don't,
I want to see fish swim, birds fly, tigers roam.
But instead of leaving them alone man is killing them
        with guns and pollution.
If you want these things just carry on the way you are going.
I'm sure you don't want all these things because I don't,
        stop killing animals.
You are putting the world in *Danger!*
I hate reading things about dead animals, they make me feel sick.
Why? Why? do we do it?

Kirsty Pearson (10) Benfieldside Junior School

Earth

Would you like to see,
the sea all black with oil?
I wouldn't.
I'd like to see the grass so green
the trees so brown, the river so blue
Wouldn't you?
Killing animals in the sea,
making acid rain,
do you know what you are doing,
stop it immediately.
soon the tropics will be black
that will be a shame,
really hoped to go there one day,
I want it to be the same.

Chris McNeil (11) Benfieldside Junior School

The Sea is Blue

The sea is blue
The grass is green
the soil is brown.
The sheds are rotting,
The birds are nesting in the trees
The peas are coming.

Paul Westgarth (10) Catchgate Primary School

Rainbow

The colours of the rainbow are beautiful and bright,
But they disappear in the darkness of the night.
The colours fade and the rainbow dies,
And waits again till the bright sky cries.

Theresa Donnelly (10) Catchgate Primary School

The Great Fire of London

Here, here the fire crunching, sizzling, roaring, banging,
                               munching all round the town.
The fire is whooshing right through the night,
dangerous, scary, horrible sight.
Horrible black smoke in the air,
some people running, they just don't care.
Smoke, ashes, sparkling flames,
around the corner just more fire,
leaping, leaping, higher and higher.
It's frightening, like lightening
lots of raging fire all over the town.

Brian Reynolds (10) Catchgate Primary School

Animals

When god made the polar bear,
He made them so that they where rare
When he made the next one he made it to that it would care.

But when he made the big blue whale,
He made it so that it was pale.
He made it so that it would sail,
Through the waters with it's tail.

And when he made a koala bear,
He made it's nose just like a square,
He made another just for a spare.

In the jungle lurks a tiger,
And it had a spider
Hiding in it's fur.

In a swamp swims a crocodile,
It's swimming down the Nile
With another crocodile.

The tortoise is a healthy thing,
It has no fur, it cannot swim
It has a very scaly back,
Of course a shell, no not a crack.

The jellyfish is a funny thing,
It stings your back in the summer swim.

The king of the jungle is a lion,
For he has such a very big iron,
He prowls around pouncing on mice
And eating them all in one gulp.

Erin Hird (8) Catchgate Primary School

Columbus's Adventure

When Columbus sailed the waters blue,
He had his troubles same as you.
For days on end
He drove his boat, before he saw the rich sands blend.
He met some Indians on the sand
He shook the chief Indians hand.
A big brown coconut fell out the tree,
It hit an Indian on the knee.
He squealed and shouted and said it hurt,
So Columbus called for the Doctor Burt.
Doctor Burt fixed his knee,
And put the coconut back up the tree.
The coconut fell out again,
And just then it started to rain.

Michael Harris (10) Catchgate Primary School

A Mouse in the Park

It was quiet, no conker hunters in sight.
A mouse scurried to and fro between a horsechestnut and oak tree.
A thick blanket of leaves carpeted the floor, while new arrivals
Fluttered to the ground.
This was the mouse's castle, split into two rooms,
Under the shade of the horsechestnut tree,
The lounge with its warm carpet of yellow and orange leaves,
And the mouse's burrowings underneath.
(Conkers are worthless to a mouse.)
Then under the spreading branches of the oak,
The kitchen with its nuts in plenty, gathered by the mouse into holes
For storage.
The mouse was happy here, at home, relaxed.
Suddenly, a noise,
The mouse pricked up its ears,
It was shouting and laughing and a stomping of feet.
The mouse froze, the noise got nearer.
The mouse stayed still.
A human appeared over the small hill in front of the two trees,
The mouse ran.
The mouse thought itself quick to dart down its hole,
But the human's eyes were quick too.
Now a new noise started up, the humans seemed to be chanting,
A mouse! a mouse!
The mouse looked up its hole,
Instead of daylight, there were lots of faces, human faces laughing
And shouting.
The mouse saw no more.
It had scurried still deeper into its hole, away from the noise and
Chaos.
Half an hour later, the mouse crept along its passage and poked its
Head out of the hole.
What it had expected.
Leaves kicked aside, all the conkers gone and the humans, having
Lost interest, gone with them.

Emma Thomas (11) Etherley Lane Primary School

Autumn in the Park

The haroh wind starts to blow,the trees
rock from side to side, as though somebody was pushing them,
making the crinkly leaves fall, rustling to the ground.
As I walk over them they crunch,
Disturbing the tranquil silence.
I was searching for brown conkers, noticing
their shells, scattered all over the ground.
I picked one up, its outside was like teeth,
ready to bite, I dropped it and it rolled away.
While finding conkers, I noticed the leaves were not
all the same, some were brown, orange, yellow and even
red, like a rainbow on the ground, not the sky.
Then as I walked to the River Gaumless, the
green wet grass beneath me, died when I stood on it,
then rose again.
Hunting for brown conkers, I noticed lots of
damp and decaying branches, snapping and
rotting beneath my feet.
On an old trees root, decomposers worked, fungi,
soft, slimy and strange.
Some larger than hands, some smaller than fingers.
Bracket fungi, weird and some looked like a
sponge.
A large, slimy, webby, amphibious frog, leaped.
Then as our time was ending, our exploring
done, we plodded back to school.
The park left, waiting for another spring, to bring
new leaves and the fresh, green grass.

Helen Cort (11) Etherley Lane Primary School

Netball

Netball is the game for me with one netball and
two posts with nets.
Fourteen girls running mad shouting and balling
as loud as they can.
*'Pass the ball to me Kate, no pass it
to me, I'm free, pass it to me. Catch the ball, to
me Nic, pass it to me Kelly, come on, shoot.'*
A long silent second that seemed like an hour. Then
all of a sudden *'Yes it went in.'*
'Good one Kristen, back to centre' said Mrs Westgarth.
It was St Mary's pass, all was quiet then a sound like a whistling
kettle, Centre threw her arms back but Alison jumped and caught
the ball she bounced passed to Gemma, Gemma passed to Sara,
Sara rolled round the top every one drew in their breath,
then it dropped threw the net.
The whistle blew Ebchester had won, the fans started singing
Ebchester C of E are the best you must agree, and that's true.

Kelly Waugh (11) Ebchester C of E Primary School

The Environment

The ozone is breaking up
But no-one is waking up,
To try to make the
World a better place for
Me and you.

All the pollution
In all of the seas.
All the cutting down
Of many of the trees.

The ozone is breaking up
But no-one is waking up,
To try to make the
World a better place for
Me and you.

Everyone uses aerosol
cans.
And give off fumes in their
Old dirty vans.

The ozone is breaking up
But no-one is waking up,
To try to make the
World a better place for
Me and you.

Kristen Kiernan (11) Ebchester C of E Primary School

The Fox

Gleaming coat, golden red, like fire
burning wild and free. Eyes as black
as coal. Razor sharp teeth that's what
a fox looks to me. Black rubbery nose
which can detect food that is hidden.
Ears that can hear a quiet rustle in
the undergrowth. Moves silent and quickly.

Ross Stoker (11) Ebchester C of E Primary School

The Badger

The badger a predator of
the night concealed in
it's dark domain through the day.
The badger silently creeping.

Kristopher Millhouse (11) Ebchester C of E Primary School

Whisper the Pony

She canters around in the night like a flashing light.
She tramples through the long damp green grass.
She stops when the sun rises in the morning.
She tosses her head and stamps her hooves,
Then canters to her hay and has a nibble.
Then her owner shouts Whisper, Whisper,
She comes to ride her in the green, green grass.

Tracey Anne Wheatley (9) Ebchester C of E Primary School

The Swan

The swan she floats so
smoothly across the moving
waters. Her feet, they move
like a dancing leaf falling
from a tree. Her children,
follow paddling behind
her, splashing with glee.

Kerry Anne Reay (9) Ebchester C of E Primary School

Raining

When it rains it runs down the wall
and onto the door, dripping and
trickling down to the ground.
Landing in a puddle with a *splash*!
Then it turns into a light drizzle,
and the sun comes out to dry
up the rain.

Sara Russell (10) Ebchester C of E Primary School

Rain! Rain!

Rain, rain what a pain, rain comes down to feed the
Drains. Rain, rain what a pain.
Sun pops up once again, the wind blew the sun away,
That's why the wind's here normally every day.
Comes here, goes there, the wind goes everywhere.
Clouds come, rain goes, clouds cover everything.

Natasha Profit (8) Ebchester C of E Primary School

A Little Hairy Monster

A little hairy monster came crawling up to me,
He walked into my bedroom and drunk my mug of tea.
He climbed into my bed and slept the night with me,
He didn't eat my breakfast instead he ate my colour
Television, so I told him to flea.

Gareth Whatson (8) Ebchester C of E Primary School

The World's Wildlife

Panda in China,
Tiger in India,
Snow white bears in Artic Ice.
Otter in England,
Whale in South Ocean,
And Elephants on African Plains.

Amy J Todd (9) Ebchester C of E Primary School

Monsterly

I have a monster in my pocket it's
red and green and really mean.
He usually lives in the trash can,
He's a real vandal man.
The trash can is rusty and split
but he doesn't care a bit.
After all he needs a home
like a dog needs a bone.
That's all now, got to go
see you next time ho, ho, ho.

Mitchell Ferwick (10) Ebchester C of E Primary School

The Slug

The slug is the biggest slimiest bug I ever saw.
It slithers and slimes until everything is covered in grime.
Oh yes, don't forget the yucky slime.
Slimy and grimy that's how the slug slithers.

Matthew Allison (10) Ebchester C of E Primary School

Rain

The
rain falls
from the
sky and
hits the
window pane.
The little drops
of water slowly
trickle down the
window and fall
onto the wall. They
slowly run down the
path. Now their journey
has ended.

Alison Day (10) Ebchester C of E Primary School

Bangs

There are bangs everywhere, everybody bangs,
even teddy bears. Whatever you do, you make bangs,
even tiptoeing across some land.
Even when you stand so really still,
a breeze will blow and you get a chill.
Sneeze, trip up and go crashing down with a *Bang!*

Andrew Gibson (9) Ebchester C of E Primary School

59

My Brother Ross

My brother Ross is thirteen years old.
Miss and he's still a beast.
Miss when he hits me with the bat.
Man walks in, Ross says she hit me with that bat.
I get the blame, but now mam knows,
Ross tricks, so now Ross gets the blame,
So that's all right.

Nicola Anderson (9) Ebchester C of E Primary School

The Owl

The owl hovers in the night sky
it is looking for a meal watching for prey.
Meanwhile on the ground, a tiny mouse scatters
about for food. It rustles the grass, the owl
swoops down. The mouse sees him at the last moment
and darts for his hole. The owl misses him by inches.
Left without a dinner, the owl will get him next time.

Peter Gibson (11) Ebchester C of E Primary School

Buttercup

Buttercup, buttercup, buttercup,
You're so sweet standing there
Beyond my feet, yellow and green,
You are a beautiful scene.

Stephen Walker (9) Tow Law School

The Night

The moon is full,
The stars shine bright.
It's time for me,
To say goodnight.
I'll close my eyes
And think of sheep,
And very soon,
I'll be fast asleep.

Catherine Taylor (9) Tow Law School

Great Fun

Great times we had,
Retirement is good, but I'll miss you.
Eager to see you again,
All missing you,
Take good care Mr Baker.
Fun we had together
Ultimate fun, it was great
Now I'm missing you.

Anthony Bennett (9) Tow Law School

Retiring

Retiring, retiring.
End of some school days,
Telling them you're leaving
'I'll miss you,' they say.
Retiring.
Ideas! You not leaving are
Not leaving, your mind tells.
Going away must be sad.

Sarah France-Sergeant (10) Tow Law School

Wintry Days

Wintry days come and go,
When they come they blow and blow.
Snow flakes falling soft and light,
That is the end of that winters sight.

Lisa Plews (10) Tow Law School

Lifting High

Lifting high,
Over clouds,
Fly high,
Tiny as a mouse.

Louise Miller (9) Tow Law School

Snow

S is for snow as light as a feather.
N is for noses in the frostiest weather.
O is for outside where the snow did lie.
W is for whiteness which falls from the sky.

Paul Murray (9) Tow Law School

Flying

Fluttering pigeons.
Low pigeons.
You can't peep.
It's impossible imagining.
Night is falling, time to sleep.
Go to sleep, not a peep.

Natalie Jacques (9) Tow Law School

Buttercup

Buttercup, buttercup in the field,
You've got a bright lovely yellow shield.
In that lovely green grass field and
Your stalk is lovely and sealed.

John Payne (9) Tow Law School

Slow Blue Flash Jesus Lazy Flying

Flight.
Light.
Yellow light.
In the air.
No more flying.
Going far away.

Spread your wings.
Low speed.
On your way.
Wing power.

Lots of time.
A lot more pigeons.
Zoom away!
Yesterday they flew.

Jesus.
Easter.
Show care.
Us like Jesus.
Show me!

Bright sight in the night.
Look over there,
Under a tree.
Eager to race.

Flight in the night,
Like yellow light
And the light is so bright.
Some pigeons are bright.
Home at last!

Robert Punshon (9) Tow Law School

Flowers

Flowers are beautiful in a special way,
I think they're pretty ok!
They come in colours red, white and blue,
Purple, orange and yellow too.
They stand in the sun,
They stand in the rain.
If anyone doesn't like flowers
They must be insane.

Louise Robinson (9) Evenwood CE Primary School

The Ghost

I've seen a ghost,
I've seen a ghost,
While sitting on the loo.
When I saw him straight away I said too-do-loo.
He looked around
And then I frowned
Because he looked so spooky.
I wish that he would go away
So I could eat my cookie

Debbie Williams (9) Evenwood CE Primary School

Rain

The rain is falling all around,
Running down the window pane,
Splashing on the ground.

Running down the guttering,
Running down the pipe,
Out onto the road and out of sight.

Catherine Hughes (9) Evenwood CE Primary School

My Dog

I have a dog his name is Ben!
He's as old as me and I'm ten!

He's black and white and some would say scruffy,
When he's not fed on time he gets quite huffy.

Although he drives me round the bend,
He's my mate, a very good friend.

Stephanie Taylor (10) Evenwood CE Primary School

A Better Place to Live

Keep Britain tidy, that's the thing to do,
When playing in the park or even at the zoo.
Use litter bins provided, come on kids play your part,
For we can build a better world, if we all get smart.

Don't throw away your paper, your bottle or empty can,
As these can all be re-used by the recycling man.
No need to chop down all the land or chop down lots more trees
And this will save the animals, the flowers, birds and bees.

So before you scatter your rubbish, make time to stop and think,
The damage to the world you are doing, by using it as a sink.
So to make us a much better future, a world that is shiny and bright,
It is not up to us and our children, so come on let's get it right.

Lorraine Tate (11) Evenwood CE Primary School

Tarzan and Monkey

Tarzan, the king of the jungle,
He swings form tree to tree,
Tarzan fell off one day and hit monkey.

Monkey is not happy,
He hit Tarzan's head,
Tarzan is very poorly, he has to go to bed.

Tarzan and monkey are friends again,
When they fight they are pretty insane,
But now they have made a promise, to keep forever,
Which is to never fight again.
Never! Ever! Ever!

Marie Robinson (11) Evenwood CE Primary School

Hallowe'en

Midnight's near and you can hear
A chanting in the sky,
Bells are pealing,
Witches squealing
And the moon is in your eyes.

It's Hallowe'en,
The clouds look mean,
All shapes of ghouls and phantoms.
Don't forget your witches hat,
Your witches cape and lanterns.

Ashley Graven (11) East Stanley Primary School

War in the World

Bang, bang, bang go the guns in the war.
Ow, ow, ow go the men in the war.
Boo, hoo, hoo go the babies in the war.
Yap, yap, yap go the men trying to stop the war.

Christopher Bell (11) East Stanley Primary School

Butterfly Mate

My mate wants to be a butterfly,
So he can roam around in the sky up high.
My mate wants to be pretty like me
And wants to look bright as well as pretty.
My mate wants to be a butterfly,
So he can glide through the sky like a glider.

Christopher Dixon (10) East Stanley Primary School

The Haunted House

The haunted house is a dark and gloomy place,
With a full moon hanging over for a light and
A graveyard for a garden, it's really an eerie house.
People say that ghosts linger in the attic and the basement,
So a word of warning, do not go near or
Even go inside the haunted house.

Jayne Waite (11) East Stanley Primary School

Living at the Greengrocers

I live in a brown crate,
Surrounded by all my friends,
Such as strawberry, lemon, apple and pear
And they all drive me around the bend.
One day when I was fast asleep
I felt myself being picked up,
When I woke up I found myself
Living in a cup.
I later found out
I was to be sold
To a greengrocer,
Who lived just along the road.
When I arrived there,
Who should I see,
But the rest of my friends
Alongside of me.
A woman came in and looked at me,
She said 'Did this gooseberry come from the sea?'
The grocer replied 'No it did not,
It came form over there, that lot.'
So the woman she bought me
And made me into jam,
What a silly idea,
She was going to put me into ham.

Amy Thirlaway (11) East Stanley Primary School

My Baby Brother

My baby brother is truly little a pain,
He cries all the time.
All the time I get the horrible jobs like changing his nappy,
Then I have to feed him.
When it is hot I take him for a walk,
Then when I come back he needs another bottle.
So I feed him and take him up stairs and put him to sleep,
Then I go back down stairs, have my supper.
I go back up stairs and go to sleep.
Then in the middle of the night I hear him crying.
It is a good job that I do not have to get up in the night and feed him,
My mam feeds him in the night.
Before I go to school I give him a kiss on the cheek.
I go to school and come home and I have to do the same jobs over
                                                                    again.
I love my baby brother.

Lucie Dixon   (11)   East Stanley Primary School

Saturn

Saturn is a great planet.
As well as all the beautiful rings
Tucked round it when it sleeps and wakes
Until it's round the sun again.
Round it goes when the sun shows.
Never stops, it goes round and round
                        until the night falls down.

Rachael Perryman (11) East Stanley Primary School

RIP

John Bunn

There was a man
Called John Bunn
Who was killed by a gun!
But his name wasn't Bunn
But another name wouldn't
Rhyme with gun.

1932-1949

God bless him

Kirsty Foggon (10) East Stanley Primary School

The Man From Japan

There was a old man form Japan
He bought a new frying pan
He cooked his eggs
And burnt his legs
And he came out with a wonderful tan.

Tanya Marie Firbank (11) East Stanley Primary School

The Mysterious Cat

In the darkness the moon is bright,
He keeps in the shadows, he doesn't like light.
When a litter bins clatter and plant pots are smashed,
Who do they blame, it's the mysterious cat.
He's always on the prowl, he comes out every night,
If you touch him you will get a fright.
He feels like nettles and smells like dirt,
If you get bitten it will really hurt.
When a litter bins clatter and plant pots are smashed,
Who do they blame, it's that mysterious cat.
When an alley has been raided, it looks a sorry sight,
He's always in mischief day or night.
He's very thin,
If he was on a rugby field, he'd be straight in the sin bin.
When a litter bins clatter and plant pots are smashed,
Who do they blame, it's that mysterious cat.

James Trow (10) Red Rose Primary School

Mouse

Creeping along is the small creature.
Tiny red eyes,
Little pink nose,
It's small fury body,
It's long pink tail,
Four tiny little feet.
It is of course
The little mouse.
When you touch it you feel it's fur,
When you look at it, you see its sorrowful eyes,
You hear its little steps as it creeps along.

Gillian Button (10) Red Rose Primary School

Solar

Sun shining down on the path to give us light.
Oil, gas and coal are all *non-renewable!*
Let's all stop global-warming *now!*
Against pollution we should be.
Renewables are the best source of *energy!*

Mark Davies (10) Red Rose Primary School

Have you Ever

Have you ever had a sore throat,
Crossed a very small moat,
Had roast duck,
Played in a great big pool of muck,
Met a teeny, weeny cat,
Called your dad and great big pratt,
Shot your mam with a gun,
Went out and had some fun,
Snapped a very long rope,
Went and met the Pope,
Sat on top of a car,
Went to your local bar?

Have you
Ever?

Phillip Stephenson (10) Red Rose Primary School

Waterfall

I am a waterfall
Alone in a park,
I have lots of friends
But now it is dark.
People throw stones at me,
Dogs drink my water,
I gurgle and splash
And I rush and dash.
I'm happy and free
And full of glee.

Stephanie Charlton (10) Red Rose Primary School

The Racoon

This strange burglar comes out every night.
He comes for food, he looks always in the dustbins.
He eats all the flowers out of the garden, everything.
This strange animal wears a mask, the racoon.
My mum always gives it food.
The racoons can smell, taste, hear, see and touch.
The creatures are sensitive.

Camille Laxton (9) Red Rose Primary School

The Snowflake

I am a snowflake,
I twist and turn, flutter and pass,
see and smell.
Racing, leaping, I jump higher and slowly,
smoothly,
I come down near to the ground.
The wind howls in the trees when
suddenly, I fall to the ground,
melting, slowly, crying, sad and then
I'm gone.

Sarah Ann Wilson (10) Red Rose Primary School

Grey Lady

Grey lady, grey lady killed herself last night
By jumping off the top of the black stairs without a single light.
So now she haunts the staircase but a single sight
When you go up or down the stairs, grey lady shivers and runs away
And she leaves a lovely smell of lavender.

Joanne Atkinson (10) Red Rose Primary School

Have you Ever?

Have you ever swam in the sea,
Been stung by a bee,
Eaten *toad in the hole,*
Climbed up a great, big pole,
Bumped your head,
Been sent to bed,
Broken a dish,
Eaten a fish,
Met Fred,
Fallen down and bled,
Sailed the sea,
Slept on a pea,
Paddled a canoe,
Seen bamboo,
Jumped on a bean,
Scrubbed yourself clean,
Painted a house,
Stood on a wood louse,
Read a book,
Loved to cook?
Have you ever?

Nikki Kimberly Wood (10) Red Rose Primary School

A Puppy

A puppy is like a ball of fur,
It looks soft
And smells of the grass outside.
It's always in mischief.
Sometimes it lies in its basket
Listening for the sound of *Walkies.*
Puppies tend to chase things
Like balls with bells inside them.
They like to be tickled and stroked
And a puppy always loves its food.

Mark Roberts (10) Red Rose Primary School

Durham

Among the mist and all the smog,
A place not even suitable for a dog,
A load of cars and a mini bus,
A lot of blood pouring from a flattened puss,
A huge Cathedral and a tiny castle,
But carrying your bag is tons of hassle,
Sheeps pumps and poos like noodles,
Because they're made with doggies doodles!
Down the river a nasty bump,
Oh my god someone's pumped!
The day is over, nearly sunset,
(Or should I put just one more pet? No!)

Stuart Rayfield (10) Red Rose Primary School

97

The Arab Stallion

He galloped on to see his mare.
His coal-black head dished and elegant.
His sleek black shadow seemed to own the world.
The Arab Stallion's big body seemed to grow with every pace
he galloped.
Racing his herd, the fiery red body of another competing Arab
Stallion drew up behind him.
The black Arab Stallion drew closer.
His mane and tail swishing and flying backwards.
He slowed to a canter, then just a trot.
He trotted cockily up to me.
I ran to meet him.
I could see him in the dark because of his white star.
I climbed onto his back and he and his herd galloped me home.
The strength of his every stride amazed me.
My black Arab Stallion nuzzled me.
I loved him even more.
His velvety nose and the whole beauty of his shining body
stunned me
And I still love him.

Jodie Surendran (10) Red Rose Primary School

98

What's in a Name

Claire is my name,
Late for school I never am,
Am very untidy at home,
I love meringues,
Rainbows and sunsets I like,
Eclairs I like.

And I love tormenting people,
Dancing is my favourite thing,
A new pair of shoes I would like,
Many things I like to eat,
Sometimes, I play out,
On my birthday I get £43.00 every year,
Never pick on my brother.

Claire Adamson (9) Red Rose Primary School

Feelings

It was *fear* for the dog *attacking* my dogs
that made me feel *frightened.*
Cleo and Jess made me feel *happy* and *excited*
when they rushed around after sticks.
Cleo made me feel *funny* when she was *daft*
on the grass.
Jess made me feel *funny* when she walked *dainty.*
They made me feel *proud* when they walk by my side,
perfectly and *loyal.*
When they lick me I feel a *buzz* inside me.
They made me feel these things because I *love* them.

Sarah Colley (10) Red Rose Primary School

Oil-Coal-Gas

Oil is non-renewable.
It is for cars.
Let us care about our world.

Coal is non-renewable.
Our world is in danger of heating up.
Ask for help and use renewable sources.
Lots of fuels are being used like oil, coal, gas.

Gas is non-renewable.
All of it is being taken for granted.
Sun shining in the sky made all these things.

Jill Sharples (10) Red Rose Primary School

Glum Mondays

Mondays are sometimes very glum,
When everyone is sleepy.

We'd rather be at home with mum
Instead of being weary.

Glum Mondays are sometimes very hard,
When we have to stay in to play.

I'd rather we outside instead,
It'll be like this all day.

The teachers leave the scissors out
So we can draw and cut.

Sometimes we make lovely things,
A house all just for us.

Sarah Rodger (11) St Benet's RC Primary School

The Herring Gull

The herring gull looks for food,
He sees a nest with an egg,
The herring gull eats the egg
And throws the shell away.

The herring gull is greedy,
He will eat anything he can,
It does not matter whose it is,
The herring gull does not mind.

Elaine Thompson (10) St Benet's RC Primary School

My Cat

My cat's slim as a pin,
She never eats anything,
She just sits as good as gold.

My cat sneaks around,
Wherever it goes
It never makes a sound.

My cat's eyes are bright
But they don't glow in the light,
They only glow in the night.

My cat will sleep anywhere,
Under a table or a chair
And she's as cuddly as a bear.

Laurie Nichol (11) St Benet's RC Primary School

My Grandfather Clock

Tick tock, tick tock,
Listen to my grandfather clock,
Watch the pendulum swaying side to side
And listen to its ticking rhyme.

Tick tock, tick tock,
Five to nine is the time,
Soon it will sing its song,
To tell the exact time.

The one bad thing about this clock
Is it keeps you awake all night long,
Tick tock, tick tock,
Ticking and telling you its song.

Oliver Sanderson (11) St Benet's RC Primary School

Mr Nobody

He trails the mud through all the house
And messes up the place.
He eats the things that you like most
Without a single trace.
He's never seen and never heard,
I guess it's up to me
To never, ever say a word
About Mr Nobody.

Tania Tunney (11) St Benet's RC Primary School

The Alley Cat

The cat is sly, slim and sleek,
Stalking around for something to eat,
He lurks in the alley ready to pounce,
This means *danger* for some little mouse.

Poor little mouse dodges around
Hoping that he will never be found,
Small and furry, mild and meek,
Will he be alive next week?

Paul Cowan (11) St Benet's RC Primary School

Snakes

Sly for comfort.
Hypnotising its prey.
Always eating alone.
Hasn't got time to stay and chat.

And you might be the next victim to
Disappear!

Colin Parmley (10) St Benet's RC Primary School

The Alley Cat

The cat scratches itself
Against the wall,
Back arched high,
Tail up tall,
Claws out long,
Nails out long,
On its toes,
Ready to stalk.

Little mouse runs
Onto the floor,
The cat comes
Closer, a little more.
Back arched high,
Tail so long,
Leaves the ground
With a little bounce,
Flying through the air,
Now on the mouse - pounce.

Philip Pallister (11) St Benet's RC Primary School

The Snake's Attack

Silently slithering up to its prey,
Its forked tongue flickers,
Its back shines during the sunny day,
Now it's ready to strike.
Its fangs are out,
It's about to bite,
It attacked, out comes the venom.
Its prey stands still,
Then it drops,
It gobbles it up and away it goes,
Silently slithering up to its next prey.

Dionne Howie (11) St Benet's RC Primary School

The Sea

The sea is a horse
With a crystal white coat
Spraying white foam
As it gallops through the ocean waves
Then back again
To rest on the golden sandy shore.

Monica-Claire Thompson (11) St Benet's RC Primary
School

Sparrow

Sparrow, sparrow
Singing sweetly,
Sparrow, sparrow
Flying high,
Sparrow, sparrow
See you later.

Sparrow, sparrow
There you are,
Sparrow, sparrow
Where are you?
Sparrow, sparrow
Have to go.

Craig Errington (11) St Benet's RC Primary School

My Cat

My cat is sly
And it wears a tie,
It goes to the town
And it clowns around.

His eyes are green
And are always seen
Flashing in the dark
As bright as a spark.

Clare Pennick (10) St Benet's RC Primary School

Fat Cat

My cat's a fast cat even though it's fat.
About to pounce it crouches low,
Wiggles its head and says yum, yum
And pounces upon the mouse.
She walks around making no sound,
At night she moves as fast as light,
Then a scruffy cat crawls up beside her,
She walks away trying to ignore her.
It pounces on her trying to gnaw her,
She frightens it away with one might blow,
She's the fattest but strongest cat I know.

Richard Gorman (11) St Benet's RC Primary School

The Fat Cat

My cat is fat, proud and tall,
It rubs itself across the wall,
If it finds a mouse
It chases it across the room.

My cat is handsome and nimble,
It could and would get you into trouble,
So beware the cat might be near.

My cat has big green eyes
Which can almost hypnotise
And at the end of the day
It curls up by the fire.

Sean Brown (10) St Benet's RC Primary School

Your Cat

Your cat can be smart,
It runs like a dart,
Watch your cat - it might scratch.

Your cat likes to roll in the puddle,
It also likes to cause a muddle,
Watch your cat - it might scratch.

Michael Scott (10) St Benet's RC Primary School

When I Grow up

When I grow up I want to be
In the RAF flying over the sea,
Or maybe in the Navy.
I might work for BOC,
I might be a Captain of a
Big ship
And sail the sea until
I'm sick.
I might be a big soccer star,
A big golf personality in par.
Whatever I'll be
I hope it suits me.

Alan Dent (10) St Benet's RC Primary School

117

Christopher Columbus

In fourteen hundred and ninety two,
Columbus sailed the ocean blue.
He asked the Spanish king and queen,
But really they were very mean.
He had to wait five years,
Until he final day occurred.
With three ships - Santa Maria the biggest of all
And the Pinta the Nina which were very small.
On the third of August he set sail,
But his rudder broke, that's his tail.
The sailors stank, they never got washed,
He then had trouble with hew crew,
Until Martin Pinzen said 'hand a few'.
The man on watch shouted 'land ahoy'
And all the crew said 'o boy'.
Columbus got off the ship and kissed the sand
And then he shouted a command.
He said search the island for gems and gold,
The treasures of Asia will now unfold.
Columbus set back for Spain
Until trouble came again.
Storms smashed the Santa Maria
And all the crew got on the Nina.
There were too many people to take home
And some people couldn't come.
So Columbus left thirty-nine behind
And he wasn't being unkind
Because they wanted to stay.
When Columbus got back, he was liked by everyone,
But a few years later he was gone.

Neil Ford (9) St Benet's RC Primary School

The Golden Dragon

A monstrous beast that lurks through the night,
It's cave isn't dirty yet clean and bright.
It looks like a dragon, its colour is gold,
Go to its cave and yet behold.
It sits on its treasure blowing out steam,
Go and see the brightest beam.
A light so still in the dark of night,
A light so still, a light so bright.
Don't be scared it does not bite,
It's my golden dragon.

Victoria Hodgson (9) St Benet's RC Primary School

My Bike

I was in my bed
With the spots, I had them head to toe
And when mum came she said you can play out
On your bike.
I was eating a pear on my bike,
A boy said to me if I was you
I would not dare to eat a pear on my bike.

So I went on,
I got to the park and sang a song,
I said I like pears do you?
Some said yes, some said no.

Sarah Peart (9) St Benet's RC Primary School

Mr Nobody

It's him who eats the ice cream
And drinks all the milk,
It's him who messes my room,
It's him who annoys the dog,
Eats the food,
Leaves the taps running,
I know who it is,
It's not me,
It's Mr Nobody.

Gemma Leigh Cooke (10) St Benet's RC Primary School

Months of the Year

January is a time of snow
As you may already know.

February is a time of ice
And it is not very nice.

March winds are very breezy
But they are sometimes teasy.

April showers are very wet
They are like a thundering jet.

May is the time of year
When sunshine may occur.

June is the month when it gets really warm
And the bees begin to swarm.

July is the time of year
When people go on holiday.

August can sometimes be cold
And your shorts are old.

September is back to school
And the weather is quite cool.

October's when the clocks go back
And it's time to wear your mac.

November is Guyfawkes night,
The fireworks are very bright.

December is when Santa comes
And brings presents by the tons.

Gina Mallon (11) St Benet's RC Primary School

The Children's Guide to Witches

Witches don't have big broom sticks or hats,
They don't even have pet vampire bats.
Those gruesome creatures look just like us,
They could even be sitting next to you on the bus.

Witches are as bold as a boiled egg,
So they wear a wig upon their head.
If you see a witch don't try to hide,
They will smell you with their nostrils wide.

A witches nails are as big as cat's claws,
So she wears her gloves wherever she goes.
So if you ever see a witch run as fast as you can go,
Then she won't catch you because she has no toes.

Laura Brown   (10) St Benet's RC Primary School

Night

Scary, quiet, worried, afraid.
I'm not scared because I'm brave.
Dark, dangerous, ghostly creaking.
Strange enchanted midnight seeking.
Alarming thoughts might make you cold.
But not me because I'm bold.

In the Dark

One night I went to bed
I saw shadows around my head,
I shouted mam, mam, then the shadow went.
It is cold.
I had nothing to hold.
I was frightened of the dark,
I heard fingernails around my head,
I thought it was a joke,
It was not, I was scared.
I cried mam, mam and the noises went.
I was frightened of the dark.

Lee Hewson (9) St Benet's RC Primary School

Christmas Tree

The shine of the lights,
The shine of the tree,
The light of the baubles shine beautifully.
The spiky needles fall to the ground
Without making very much sound.
Colourful, bright, spiky and blue,
All the light shines over you.
Sparky, prickly, shining with green,
Our lady on top becomes the queen.

Mark Ward (9) St Benet's RC Primary School

My Planet

My planet is funny
When some people jump like bunny's,
Girls dress as boys and boys like girls.

My house there
Has candy bricks,
Chocolate walls
And lollipop doors.

My car there
Has strawberry and cherry ice cream doors,
Sugar for the windows.

Scott Noble (9) St Benet's RC Primary School

Pollution

People dump litter
And they don't care.
They smoke and pollute the air.
Oil is spilled into the sea,
On beaches where it should not be.
It kills the birds, seals and fish
And poisons others that could land on our dish.

Peter Daglish (10) St Benet's RC Primary School

My World

My world has chocolate for the walls
And jelly for the doors,
Lollies for the lamp post.
                    My world is strange.

My land is topsy turvey sometimes,
People wear their shoes on their hands.
                    My world is strange.

My car is made out of candy,
The glass is made out of sugar.
                    My world is strange.

Andrew Simpson (10) St Benet's RC Primary School

Sounds in the House

The washing machine is on,
My brother's watching TV,
My dad came in from work,
My dog is barking loudly,
My mam is making the tea
The only quiet one is me.
                    Outside.

I heard a owl hoot in darkness and a
Cat prowling and a dog barking, I
Was worried so I hurried to the window
To see if it was a full moon,
It was, I hope morning soon.

Gary Holden (10) St Benet's RC Primary School

Columbus

In 14 hundred and 92,
Columbus sailed the ocean blue,
He asked the king and queen of Spain,
But all he got for his trouble was pain.
In five years he asked again,
He hoped to find his fortune and fame,
Columbus said thank you.
All I need now is some crew.
The Pinzon brothers are coming with me,
We're going to sail over the sea.
He got some trouble with the crew,
Until he said hang a few,
We reached an island safe at last,
We got off the ship very fast.
On the way back there was a storm,
But after that it was sunny and warm.
When Columbus got back to Spain
He got his fortune and his fame.

John Soulsby (9) St Benet's RC Primary School

Animals And the Environment

Save the animals in the jungle,
Save the animals in the zoo,
Save the animals that are hunted,
Save the animals that are dying,
Love the animals that love you.

Stop making the pollution,
Stop cutting down the trees,
Stop killing animals in the sea,
Stop cutting down the jungle,
Because it could kill you and me.

Try stopping air pollution,
Try not throwing things in the sea,
Try to stop polluting the air we breath,
Try not to kill the lands animals,
It could kill you and me.

Kirsty-Anne Harrison (9) St Benet's RC Primary School

Columbus

In fourteen hundred and ninety two
Columbus sailed the ocean blue,
He sailed with a crew
On a boat that was new.
He sailed to Asia to look for gold,
To make this trip he must have been bold.
He landed at last upon some sand
Hispaniola he called this land.
The Indians gave him a mask of gold,
He took it home so it could be sold,
He sold it for one hundred coins of gold,
By now Columbus was getting old.

Stephanie Nicholson (10) St Benet's RC Primary School

In the Dark

Shadows on my wall,
Noises like ghosts,
I lie in my bed all afraid,
It's very·quiet, not a sound but I'm still very scared.
A shadow is lurking over there,
I shout mum 'I'm really scared.'
She shouts up 'I don't really care, now try and get to sleep.'
But I can't, I know I can't.
I lie their shivering,
Then I hear a noise, I am very alarmed,
I nearly jump out of my skin.
Then all the lights go out,
All in the street too,
I scream I'm scared,
My mum runs up,
We've had a power cut.

Victoria Thomas (10) St Benet's RC Primary School

Columbus

In fourteen hundred and ninety two
Columbus sailed the ocean blue,
He went to the queen to ask for money
But the queen said 'no', she thought that he was funny.
Then after a while they all said
'Yes, oh thank you Sir, I am impressed.'

Then he went to find his crew,
Not a lot, just a few.

Then after a while there came a great storm
But there was no harm.

So they went on to find land,
Finally they came to some sand
And they thought it was grand
And that's what happened in fourteen hundred and ninety two.

Maddalena Cultrera (10) St Benet's RC Primary School

School

I can hear the teacher talking
But I can feel my mind a walking,
Walking off to dreamers land.
Falling asleep is close at hand,
Although it is very noisy
With children talking.
Adults walking
Round and round.
Now I know that we are bound
Not to make a single sound,
Now it's near the end of the day,
When we get outside we'll shout hooray!
School!

Alexandra Nelson (10) St Benet's RC Primary School

Christopher Columbus

In fourteen hundred and ninety-two
Columbus sailed the ocean blue,
When they shouted land ahoy
All the people went 'oh boy'.
But the land was just a cloud,
The sailors formed an angry crowd,
The captain wasn't very proud,
To mutiny they weren't allowed.
All they could drink was water and wine
While for land they searched for a land sign.

Robin Kent (10) St Benet's RC Primary School

School Sounds

It's Friday and I'm in bed,
Sounds of school are in my head.

In school my favourite thing is work,
Today my throat is sore, I can hardly talk.

My best friend is Gemma Cooke,
Oh, how she loves to drop her maths book.
Now sounds like talking can be heard,
Do you want to know how to spell a word?
As the computer goes *beep,*
Yet I am nearly asleep.

Shouting, screaming, playground bell,
Oh, who is the big mouth we can't tell.
On and on the sounds they go,
Now some are high and some are low.
When is it Monday?

Katy Walls (10) St Benet's RC Primary School

Mr Nobody

He's the one who smashed the window
And put skates on the stairs,
Then burst the tyres on the car
And shredded all the spares.
He swung the cat around his head,
Then ruined the TV,
The vase was smashed by no-one else
But Mr Nobody.

He mixed up all the paint colours
And drew on all the walls,
He ripped up our best story books
And popped my favourite ball.
He gets my toys and leaves them out,
He made my sister cry,
But it is never us you see,
It's Mr Nobody.

Stephen Nicholson (11) St Benet's RC Primary School

Our Cat

When our cat was only small
He used to play upon the wall,
He had sharp claws and very sly eyes
And raided a cupboard once in a while!

When our cat was allowed outside
He began to wander far and wide,
He prowled through gardens climbing trees,
But who could guess what he could see?

Now our cat is older still
And doesn't play on the window sill,
But sits next to the comforting fire
And goes to sleep when we retire.

Catherine Catwell (11) St Benet's RC Primary School

Herring Gull

Gulls diving in the sea
To get some fish for their tea.
The fish must dive to stay alive,
If they don't they will die.
On the cliffs the sea gulls nest,
That is where they come to rest,
Sitting down to hatch their brood,
Taking turns to bring back food.
When the little birds arrive,
Back to work and time to dive.

Mark Richardson (11) St Benet's RC Primary School

The Alley Cat

I see the cat, shiny of eye,
Moving so nimbly, sharp and sly.
It keeps to the shadows, dark and silent,
Then goes to kill with claws so violent.

Its handsome eyes shine so brightly,
When it walks, it paces lightly.
This nimble feline has a playful side,
So many talents far and wide.

A little mouse has no chance
As the cat begins to advance,
Its razor sharp glare remains unshifted
As this unlucky rodent is lifted
Into the jaws of the meriless cat,
It will become a dinner time snack.

Christopher Scott (11) St Benet's RC Primary School

Snakes

Snakes curl themselves round and round,
Listen carefully to their hissing sound.
Snakes normally come out at night.
Beware of where you step
Because it will bite.
Their skin is smooth,
But watch out when it's on the move.
If you touch their skin it feels dry.
But some people think they are very sly.

Viktoria Smith (11) St Benet's RC Primary School

Snakes Are Everywhere

One day I walked into my store
I saw a snake upon my door.
I picked it up, it was shiny and dry,
I thought it would have been slimy.

Lee Miller (10) St Benet's RC Primary School

Clear Waters

The river was clear,
It was crystal clear like glass
On a full moon night.

Craig Ackerley (10) Lamplugh School

Mr Table Called Mable

I have a table her name is Mable,
She likes to eat cables
And lives in a stable,
That's my table called Mable.

Stuart Christie (10) Lamplugh School

Herons And Kingfisher

One winter morning the air was cold
And snow on the ground,
The heron was fishing
In the cold beck.
There was hardly any fish.
In the pond near the house
Was a kingfisher,
A good friend to the heron, sometimes
They go fishing together.
Sometimes they're lucky,
Sometimes they're not.
The best catch for heron
Was two trout
And for kingfisher was fifteen minnows.
They still are friends
Whatever they catch.

Alan Strong (10) Lamplugh School

The Beast's Final Morn

In the new light of a fresh morn, off yonder hills the beast emerged
To bring immortal suffering to the villagers,
Not only to the beast's prey
But to the beloved ones of the unfortunate sole.
Just then the beast made an unearthly howl
And lumbered clumsily down the hill side
And made its violent lurch on top of a lonely villager
Who was fleeing for her life.
Just then a strange figure was spied
In the shadow of a bank,
The figure stepped out,
For 'twas a man with anger in his eyes.
A woman came, pulled at his arm trying to persuade him not to go,
Just then the beast looked up for he had seen a light
Glistening off the young man's sword,
For after came a horrific battle,
The beast against the boy.
It became worse and worse,
Then they lay the beast also the boy,
The girl wept,
The people didn't know what to do, laugh or cry.
The boy was dead, the beast was dead,
They were both slayed by each other.
The woman went to the lad's body,
Lay down peacefully on his chest and died with him in peace,
For it had been true love
And now in heaven they shall meet.

Matthew Dowding (11) Lamplugh School

The Kangaroo Poem

When I got up my face went blue
To see a kangaroo
Hopping round the garden
On its two feet.
Fell down a hole
And had to have false teeth.
The doctor came,
Clip clop
His new shoes went
On the block.
Ring ring
At the door,
Went in
And fell down another hole.

Gemma Ross (9) Lamplugh School

Mr Platypus

Mr Platypus got on a bus
Smoking a hammered cigar,
He coughed and spluttered
And then he muttered
I think I'll buy a car.

The next day
Mr Platypus jumped on his car
Eating a hammered cigar,
He coughed and spluttered
And then he muttered
I think I'll eat my car.

Alexa Mottram (10) Lamplugh School

Mr Friend

My friend is called Harry, he's very mad
And he's got a wig, or at least he had.

He is six foot tall, wears size twelve shoes
And he is crazy on kangaroos.

He says everything is mental
And he never eats lentils.

Philip Grech (10) Lamplugh School

The River

The river is calm and crystal clear.
The river is cold and very deep.
The river has small and big fish
Swimming around in it.

Michael Shield (10) Lamplugh School

Water Project

Save water people.
Don't waste paper.
Did you hear me?

Adam Ross (11) Lamplugh School

Water Changing

Water flows like silk, it runs like spilling milk.
Water is rough, tough, rippling, rugged.
Water is so calm, it won't do any harm.

Daniel Hayton (10) Lamplugh School

Stop Smoking

Now this is a story all about why if
You smoke you will most likely die.
Because when you smoke a fag it's
Got you in the bag.
When you have a fag people
Think that you're a slag!
Smoking's not cool, don't be a fool.
When you smoke those fags your
Lungs inflate like bags!
When you smoke at the bar your
Lungs end up like tar.
So when you smoke in the corners
Your lungs end up like saunas.
So please don't smoke.

Daniel Gullon (10) Lamplugh School

The Crystal Clear Water

The sun is rising,
The water is crystal clear,
Clear, clear through the day.

Douglas Pembleton (10) Lamplugh School

Waste

Water drips and slops,
The water goes down the drain,
Wasted forever.

Philip Jackson (11) Lamplugh School

Where's the Water

Running down the hill.
Flowing freely like the wind.
Running down the hill.

Laura Smith (11) Lamplugh School

Water Here, Water There

Water glides sweetly,
Flowing past the hill side path,
Water glides sweetly.

Rachel Wilson (11) Lamplugh School

Water Water

Calm running water,
Running around the country
Very quietly.

Erica Youds (11) Lamplugh School

Water Water

Down the stream.
Flowing up and down.
Silky as can be.

Louise Shield (9) Lamplugh School

The Killer

Mother strong, so is baby,
In their nest feeding freely,
Getting ready to take off,
Hungry hunter,
Teasing others,
Young but strong.

Every one admires him
And other birds fear him,
Games and fun are all for the eagle,
Leaning over his craggy rock,
Eager to dive for the kill.

Jennie Payne (9) Old Hutton School

Raindrops

listen to the rain,
listen to it pattering on the roof,
listen to it pounding on the ground,
listen to it coming down the chimney.

watch the rain,
watch it forming puddles,
watch it pouring down the gutter,
watch it dripping on the trees.

The rain makes me happy,
The rain makes me sad,
The rain feeds crops,
The rain feeds us.

The rain makes pictures,
It makes floods,
It makes a mirror image,
It makes streams flow with speed.

Rain can be beautiful,
The dew on the grass,
Dew on spiders webs,
Rain makes beautiful waterfalls.

William Morton (10) Old Hutton School

Chris the Little Old Tramp

Old,
Old,
Is Chris the tramp.
Chris, ·
Chris,
With a can of beer
And without fear,
His hair is like tatty string.
Nice,
Nice,
Is Chris, his family want him to live with them,
But he will not go,
A bowl is a tin for him,
But still when I see him I say 'Hello'
And he says 'Hello' to me.

Maria Holliday (10) Brook Street Primary School

The Butcher

He stands in the shop with his long, grey beard.
With his deep brown eyes he stares at you as you come through the
door.
He wears a long coat as he stands behind the counter
And his brown, old hat slips off his head.
He's a nice old man but he is shy when he sees anyone.
When he's not working he sits in a field watching the ducks on the
pond,
When he's done he sighs and walks slowly home.

Philip Coulter (11) Brook Street Primary School

Untitled

I have brought you a crystal ball so you can have wisdom.
I have brought you a knight so you will be brave and have courage.
I have brought you a coin to bring you wealth.
I have brought you a glass so you can have beauty.
I have brought you a bear so you will be comforted.
I have given you a heart so you will love.
I have brought you a friend so you will have friendship.
I have brought you silver to bring you luck.
I have brought you paper so you will have intelligence.
I have brought you a book so you will have knowledge.
I have brought you a fish to make sure you don't go hungry.
I have brought you a blanket to keep you warm.

Micheyla White (11) Brook Street Primary School

Red

A deep, bloody pain,
Or a hot, blazing fire,
Like a joyful laugh full of love.
Hot steam rising from a sizzling pan,
The sunset setting over the street,
Or the cry from the war.

Elizabeth Atkinson (10) Brook Street Primary School

Eyes

I am looking at you
And watching you,
I can view you
In the distance
And see you.

I am spying on you
And staring at you,
Peeping at night
In your bedroom.
Look through your keyhole,
Tomorrow night.

Stephen Skinner (11) Brook Street Primary School

Eyes

To stare, spy, scan, seek or search,
To watch,
To gaze, to glare, to glance, to grasp,
To view,
To inspect,
To behold with amazement,
To understand.

Danny Power (10) Brook Street Primary School

Eyes

Look,
Looking and seeing,
Glancing at someone,
Glaring and staring at my book,
Examining some clues,
Peeping at your work,
But best of all watching the time go by.

Vanessa Hull (10) Brook Street Primary School

Eyes

People glaring,
People staring,
People searching all over the place.
People peeping,
People spying,
People gazing all over the place.
People looking,
People watching,
People glancing all over the place.

And that's what eyes can do.

Christopher Sheckley (10) Brook Street Primary School

Cream

A pearl in an oyster, the sand and a shell,
Some landscape, a painting, the ring in a bell.
A baby, some softness, the opening to peace,
A country, some patience, the hotness in Greece.
A wedding, a cake, some fish in the sea,
A bird in the sky and a young child's glee.

Emily Winter (10) Brook Street Primary School

Chris

Old,
Old,
Is Chris.
Chris,
His hair all tangled,
His hands are scarred,
His face is browned,
He wears such tatty shoes,
His shirt half in, half out,
His pants are torn at the knee,
His hat is woollen and maybe torn.
Chris,
Chris,
He's sad,
He's lonely.

Jennifer Jefferson (10) Brook Street Primary School

Wildlife

Save all animals, great and small,
Don't let people kill animals for the skin,
Try to save animals.
Don't let people chop off the elephants' tusks,
Let the animals live.
I don't want people to kill animals,
I want animals to live.

Simon Calvert (9) Cotehill C of E Primary School

Weekdays

Monday kills the fish, the sharks and the crabs,
Everything in the sea.

Tuesday kills the sheep and cattle,
Not enough food to go around.

Wednesday the electricity dies,
We have used it up.

Thursday pollution comes and kills the bugs,
The beetles and the flies.

Friday gets the birds, the monkeys,
The lions and the elephants.

Saturday kills the trees, the planets and
The oxygen, that means our world will die.

Sunday, humans have destroyed the Earth,
There's no one to blame but themselves.

Beth Dunant (10) Cotehill C of E Primary School

Whales

Men are going out in boats
Just to kill the whales,
The whales are getting killed just for meat and soap,
We don't know why they do it, probably just for fun as well.
People sell the meat then they get the money,
The money feeds their families,
But the whales don't get anything,
The whales don't like being killed, the men wouldn't like it either.
They wouldn't like it if the whales jumped out the water with a
                              harpoon and shot them in the back.

Mark Pimlott (11) Cotehill C of E Primary School

When Will it Stop?

When will it stop? The people say,
The killing of thousands of animals every day.

Tigers, whales, dolphins, elephants and all,
They don't care, they'll kill them all.

When will it stop? They'll soon be extinct,
But some people just don't think.

Animals are just like us,
But once they're killed
There'll be no time to make a fuss.

Except the memories
Of the cries,
Of those who live no
More!

Hayley Graham (11) Cotehill C of E Primary School

Wildlife

Water gushing out of their mouths, drowning whales.
Ivory from elephants making ornaments out of their tusks.
Living elephants hunters killing them every day.
Dying whales making them into soap and meat.

Ladies wear tiger skin coats.
Iron harpoons fired to kill whales.
Fur coats made out of animals skin.
Every day animals suffer for money.

Ryan Atkinson (9) Cotehill C of E Primary School

Wildlife

Men shoot elephants for their tusks
And make fancy stuff.
Men in boats shoot whales with harpoon guns
And make soap, oil and food.
Men shoot tigers for their skin
And make coats for rich ladies.
This makes me feel angry and sad.

Neil Dickinson (9) Cotehill C of E Primary School

Our Forests

Our forests are going fast,
It's up to us to make them last.
Destroying animals' homes all over the land,
It's up to us to get it banned.
Trees are going one by one,
Soon there will be not one, but none
Bringing on cattle everyday.
We need a good battle to keep them away.
So, you see, this deforestation needs to stop,
We need your help, we need it a lot.

Kelly Johnstone (10) Cotehill C of E Primary School

Bye Bye

When the elephants in a group
Go past some trees
With a hunter in them
Bang!
Goes his gun.
He may miss this time
But he will try again,
He waits until another herd comes around
Bang!
He's got one.
He's cut off the tusks
And maybe will kill a few more,
The tusks are made into jewellery
Necklaces, bracelets and earrings.
So when you are out
Wearing the fancy earrings and necklaces
Just think,
It cost a life to make them!
While you are out
Having fun,
The elephant
Is lying
Dead!

Sarah Johnston (9) Cotehill C of E Primary School

Stop Killing the Whales

Don't kill the whales for blubber and oil,
Whales are mammals they have feelings as well,
Whales don't like being chased for miles and miles,
Why don't you let them have a smile?

Stop killing the whales for blubber and oil,
Soon they will be extinct,
You can't cook them in foil,
So keep them alive, forever.

David Patton (10) Cotehill C of E Primary School

Destruction

Stop dumping waste in the ocean,
Don't let the gases ruin the air,
Barely any beaches left clean from radiation,
You're slowly but surely ruining the earth.

Stop making missiles,
Atomic and nuclear,
You're causing lots of destruction,
Tons of it each day.

One day in the future
There'll be no-one left,
No more generations,
Everything will be dead.

Paul Atkinson (11) Cotehill C of E Primary School

Whaling

Whale
Swimming,
Harpoon
Pointed. Harpoon
Shot. Blood
Pouring!
Electricity pole
Jabbed, pain,
Death!
Rhino
Eating, gun aimed, bullet
Shot. Blood, pain,
Dead. Horn cut off,
Left to rot.
Elephants,
Grey, charging.
Gun loaded.
Bullet,
Shot,
Death,
Tusk cut
Off.
Left to rot.

Robert Bainbridge (9) Cotehill C of E Primary School

War

Nuclear bombs and radiation sickness,
People dead.
Mushroom cloud, fire and acid rain
Affecting crops.
People are bleeding and hurt,
The world polluted.

John Bainbridge (9) Cotehill C of E Primary School

Jungle

Parrots, elephants,
Crocodile shoes,
All things expensive,
All things to loose.
Fox, red and fluffy,
You shoot it,
It dies.
Then you make it
Into a prize.
It may be a coat,
It may be a scarf,
You want it,
Dead
Or alive.
You want it,
Greed, just greed.

Laura Mackinnon (9) Cotehill C of E Primary School

The Last Bird

When the last parrot
Gets shot
For the beauty and elegance
Of its feathers,
To be
Or not to be
A fan.
When the last swallow
Flies to the south,
It's mother and father are stuffed.
When the last crow is shot and hung, it's beak
low, it's brain all dumb.
What will be left? A sad, sad world.

Lucy Foster (9) Cotehill C of E Primary School

Kids

Who needs kids, what are they for?
They come hounding.
They say they are bored.
They say they are nice and sweet,
So you have to give them a treat.
If they don't get their own way
They will sit and sulk all through the day.

John Carroll (11) Abbotsmead Junior School

Animals

Fox hunting for his dinner,
If he can't find anything
He'll get thinner.
Kangaroo jumping so high,
I think
He will touch the sky.
Grizzly bears, strong and tall,
I think they could smash a wall.

Daniel Hughes (9) Blackford C of E Primary School

Bacon

The frying pan
With the bacon in
Is my target,
I am the bacon thief,
I love bacon
For my supper.

Craig Airey (9) Blackford C of E Primary School

Football

Football is an exciting sport
A lot of children have been taught,
They want to play for England one day,
Hopefully on a Wednesday
Because they wanted to see
How good they looked on TV.

Christopher Scott (10) Blackford C of E Primary School

The Tiger

In the jungle where it's hot
The tiger looks for its tea,
If he can't find anything
His tea could be me.

The tiger is orange and black,
He slithers through the grass,
His track leads to a den
Where there's tigers in groups of ten.

Daniel Slee (9) Blackford C of E Primary School

Trees

I love my big fat tree
With green, green leaves and a dark brown trunk,
With big red apples, I really like my tree.

Jonathan Brown (11) Blackford C of E Primary School

Taj Mahal

The Taj Mahal is a wonderful place,
Full of silk and full of lace,
While visitors sit on royal stools
The Rajah's having a splash in the pool!
Cameras clicking all around
Not only at the palace, also at the grounds.

James Wilson (9) Blackford C of E Primary School

To a Guinea Pig

'I want a guinea pig' I wined,
A little, furry guinea swine!

On and on I would implore,
Mum's patience couldn't stand much more!

Until one day she just gave in,
Threw in the towel, dropped the pin!

A guinea pig it was to be,
So we went into town, just mum and me.

When we got to the pet shop, gosh what a load!
So many little guinea pigs in sawdust abode.

I looked at the guinea pigs sitting in their cages,
By the time that I had chosen one, we had been there ages!

He looked so peaceful lying there upon his little bed,
So I thought that I would wait a while and get a dog instead!

Rose Bell (10) Blackford C of E Primary School

On the Farm

Red faced farmer's wife making dinner
Goes to open the door, leaves the soup on to simmer.

Furry kitten thirsty for milk
Sees his mother, runs off full tilt.

At half past five the farmer's ready for anything,
Sees the soup on simmer and sits down for his dinner.

Farmer looks wistfully out of the window at
His daughter's boyfriend and so at six o'clock
Dinner is served, seconds or even thirds.
A few hours later up to bed, everyone proceeded
After hot milk was needed. So until the morning
The house is quiet until the dawning.

Kitty McDarby (10) Blackford C of E Primary School

A White Horse

A wild pony gallops freely along the beach,
The sun reflecting like a mirror off its smooth coat.
Its mane and tail like a clear mountain stream as it blows behind it in
the wind.

It gallops along the shallow edge of the sea.
Splashing water high into the air,
It goes through an arch and up a hill and is gone,
What a wonderful feeling it must be to be free.

Kris MacKay (11) Blackford C of E Primary School

My Mum

When my mum is cross her eyebrows form over her eyes like storm
clouds.
Then the storm strikes . . .

Her lips go all tight as she speaks, her voice like a roll of thunder.

And in a flash the plate goes crashing down onto the table with a
thud, the same way fork lightening displays it's might by crashing into
an unfortunate victim . . .

Then the storm subsides as my mum moves towards the kitchen like
a storm moving to give another town a taste of water.

If you go into the kitchen then you are caught in the storm again like
a poor traveller in the wild, trying to find an Inn to spend the night.

It takes hours for the storm to fully subside, as with my mum, but
next day the sun is shining.

Andrew Gallie (11) Gosforth C of E Primary School

I Asked my Gran

On Monday after school, we went to visit Gran.
We had been very busy working about prehistoric things.

I said Gran, what's a Tyrannosaurus Rex?
What, you have a hole in your dress!
Did you tear it on the chest?

Then I said Gran, what a Protoceratops?
What, you would like some 'jelly tots'?
Oh go on then, look in one of my sweetie pots.

Gran what is a Diplodocus?
What you're feeling hopeless, don't be depressed.

Then I shouted when it is time for tea?
Don't shout said Gran, anyone would think I was deaf.
I'm only 103.

Sarah Lowis (9) Bellvue Junior School